The month of March, from the illuminated manuscript *Les Trés Riches Heures du duc de Berry*

The Story of a Special Day
Volume 87

March

27

86th day of the year
(87th in leap years)
279 days remaining
until the end of the year.

by Michael Dobson

Timespinner Press

Table of Contents

Cover: Japanese cherry trees blooming during the National Cherry Blossom Festival, with the Washington Monument in the background — for the Event of the Day.

Milton Berle

March 27 Quotations

"I did not think; I investigated."

Wilhelm Röntgen, discoverer of x-rays, born March 27, 1845

"God is in the details."

Ludwig Mies van der Rohe, architect, born March 27, 1886

"A leader has to appear consistent. That doesn't mean he has to be consistent."

James Callaghan, British prime minister, born March 27, 1912

"It's always the good men who do the most harm in the world."

Henry Adams, historian, died March 27, 1918

"Orbiting Earth in the spaceship, I saw how beautiful our planet is. People, let us preserve and increase this beauty, not destroy it!" (Облетев Землю в корабле-спутнике, я увидел, как прекрасна наша планета. Люди, будем хранить и приумножать эту красоту, а не разрушать её!)

Yuri Gagarin (Юрий Гага́рин),cosmonaut, first human to journey into outer space, died March 27, 1968

"I'm 83, and I feel like a 20-year-old, but unfortunately there's never one around."

Milton Berle, comedian, died March 27, 2002

Blooming cherry trees along the Tidal Basin, Washington, DC

National Cherry Blossom Festival

On March 27, 1912, First Lady Helen Herron Taft and Viscountess Iwa Chinda, wife of the Japanese Ambassador to the United States, planted the first two of over 3,000 Japanese cherry trees donated by the city of Tokyo, Japan, along the north bank of the Tidal Basin in Washington, DC, culminating a 27-year old effort to bring cherry trees to the nation's capital.

The idea of planting cherry trees in Washington came from Eliza Ruhamah Scidmore, the first female board member of the National Geographic Society. Her first attempts to interest people in the beautiful *sakura no hana* (桜の花), as cherry blossoms are known in Japanese, met with little success, but in 1906, plant explorer Dr. David Fairchild planted a hundred cherry trees on his Chevy Chase property to test their hardiness and suitability to the Washington, DC, climate. Cherry trees began to sprout all over the Chevy Chase area. Mrs. Scidmore wrote the First Lady, the wife of William Howard Taft, who had herself lived in Japan and knew the trees well. By coincidence, Jokichi Takamine (高峰 譲吉), discoverer of adrenaline, was in Washington in the company of the Japanese consul. When Takamine learned of the plan, he offered 2,000 trees to be donated as a gift from the city of Tokyo.

Sadly, the original gift of trees turned out to be infected with insects and had to be burned. Another donation, this time of 3,000 trees, was successful. The United States in turn donated flowering dogwood trees to Japan. The beauty of the trees made them an instant hit, and starting in 1935, the nation's capital began the annual Cherry Blossom Festival.

Shortly after the Japanese attack on Pearl Harbor in 1941, four cherry trees were found cut down, presumably in response to the attack. For the duration of the war, the cherry trees were referred to as "Oriental" rather than "Japanese," and the Cherry Blossom Festival was suspended until 1947. The cherry tree grove in Tokyo from which the American stock had been drawn was diminished by the war, so in 1952 the United States sent budwood from its trees back to Japan.

In 1965, the Japanese gave another 3,800 cherry trees to the United States. First Lady Lady Bird Johnson and wife of the Japanese Ambassador Ryuji Takeuchi reenacted the original planting ceremony to mark the occasion.

There are twelve varieties of Japanese cherry trees planted along the Tidal Basin. The two most common are the Yoshino, which produces single white blossoms, and the Kwanzan, which produces clusters of clear pink double blossoms. Other varieties include the Akebono, with single pale pink blossoms; Fugenzo, with rosy pink double blossoms; and Shirofugen, white double blossoms that turn pink.

Today, more than 700,000 people each year visit Washington, DC, for the two-week National Cherry

Blossom Festival. The celebration include a kite festival, event celebrating Japanese culture and heritage, bike tours, a fireworks exhibition, a ten-mile run, the Cherry Blast festival, and the culminating event, the National Cherry Blossom Festival Parade.

Blossoming Yoshino Sakura cherry tree,
Tidal Basin, Washington, DC

March 27 Holidays and Celebrations

Tatmadaw Nei (Armed Forces Day) (Burma)

March 27 is celebrated in Burma as Armed Forces Day. It was previously called Resistance Day, marking resistance to the Japanese occupation in 1945.

National "Joe" Day (United States)

On National "Joe" Day, everyone has the right to be known as "Joe" for the day, regardless of your real name. Like many of these made-up holidays, the origin of National "Joe" Day is obscure, but it has gained in popularity, at least as measured by Internet and Facebook articles.

National Spanish Paella Day (United States)

In the United States, almost every day of the year is dedicated to a particular food. Sponsored by manufacturers, retailers, farmers, or simply fans, these days are often proclaimed by the President, Congress, state governors, or mayors. March 27 is National Spanish Paella Day. Paella is a saffron rice dish to which various things are added: seafood, meats, beans, vegetables, and other ingredients.

World Theatre Day (International)

Established in 1961 by the International Theatre Institute, March 27 is celebrated as World Theatre Day. Special theatrical events take place around the world. Each year, an outstanding figure in theater shares his or her reflections on theatre and international harmony. The message is translated into more than twenty languages and read aloud before tens of thousands of spectators in different locations.

Christian Feast Days

In *Western Christianity*, saints commemorated on March 27 include Amador of Portgal, Augusta of Treviso, Gelasius, John of Egypt, Romulus of Nîmes, Rupert of Salzburg, and Zanitas and Lazarus of Persia.

In *Eastern Orthodox Christianity*, it is the commemoration of the Icons of the Most Holy Theotokos, Glykophylousa, and of the Akathist, and the Repose of Elder Augustine of Philotheou. Commemorated saints include the John the Clairvoyant, Paphnutius of Thebes, Paul the Standard Bearer, Ephraim of Rostov, and Ambrose the Confessor. (These are celebrated on April 9 by "Old Calendarists.")

USS Constitution, one of the original six US Navy frigates,
in Boston Harbor, 2006

What Happened on March 27?

1794 – The United States Establishes a Permanent Navy

The colonial-era Continental Navy was disbanded following the American Revolutionary War because the newly independent United States was broke. However, piracy against American merchant ships in the Mediterranean Sea became an increasing problem, and in response the US Congress passed the Naval Act of 1794 on March 27 of that year, authorizing the construction of the original six frigates of the United States Navy. The cost was $688,888.82, which is roughly the equivalent of $35 billion in 2012 dollars.

1836 – Goliad Massacre

On March 27, 1836 (twenty-one days after the Battle of the Alamo), the Mexican Army executed over 300 Republic of Texas soldiers taken prisoner near Goliad, Texas, by direct order of Mexican President Antonio Lopez de Santa Anna, who hoped to end the Texas rebellion against Mexican rule. Just under a month later, the Texas War of Independence would end in Santa Anna's defeat at the Battle of San Jacinto.

1884 – Cincinnati Courthouse Riots

Public outrage at a manslaughter verdict in a clear case of murder began with attacks against jurors in the trial and an attempt to find and lynch the defendants. Over the next few days, over 50 people would die in one of the most destructive riots in American history.

1915 – Typhoid Mary is Quarantined

Mary Mallon (also known as Mary Brown), a cook and later a laundress, was the first known asymptomatic carrier of the salmonella bacteria that causes typhoid fever. While she herself showed no symptoms of the disease, people with whom she came into contact would become infected — at least 50 such victims were known, including three who died.

Born in Ireland, she emigrated to the United States at the age of fifteen. Typhoid researcher George Soper first linked Mary Mallon to outbreaks of typhoid fever in at least seven locations where she worked. She was quarantined for three years and released in exchange for an agreement that she would stop being a cook. However, she went back on her word, and after a major outbreak at a hospital where she worked, police chased her down and on March 27, 1915, she was put back into quarantine, where she lived until her death in 1938.

1977 – Tenerife Airport Disaster

On Sunday, March 27, 177, the deadliest accident in aviation history took place on Tenerife, the largest of Spain's Canary Islands.

The chain of events was set in motion when a bomb set by Canary Island separatists went off in the main Canary Island airport at Gran Canaria. Incoming flights were diverted to the smaller regional airport at Tenerife, which was quickly overwhelmed by the unaccustomed volume of traffic. Worse, a dense fog compromised visibility.

Without ground radar, the air traffic controllers were unable to see the positions of the aircraft. Two Boeing 747s, KLM Flight 4805 (carrying 248 passengers) and Pan Am Flight 1736 (carrying 396 passengers), taxied toward the single runway. A series of miscommunications led to the KLM flight trying to take off while the Pan Am flight was still on the runway. The collision destroyed both 747s, killing everyone on the KLM flight and all but 61 on the Pan Am flight.

This disaster resulted in an overhaul of communications protocols and other changes to avoid a repetition.

Computer-generated reconstruction of the collision of two Boeing 747s at Tenerife

1980 – Silver Thursday

Billionaire brothers Nelson and William Hunt attempted to
corner the market in silver, and acquired more than a third
of all the silver held outside government coffers
worldwide, borrowing heavily to do so. Prices climbed
from $6/ounce to nearly $50/ounce. Because of the Hunt
brothers' move, the rules on buying commodities on
margin were changed, and when the price of silver
collapsed on March 27, 1980, they received a margin call
for $100 million, which they could not meet. The resulting
panic threatened the existence of several large banks and
brokerage firms, which were saved by a consortium of
banks. The brothers lost over a billion dollars directly,
were convicted of civil charges of conspiracy, and were
forced to declare bankruptcy in one of the biggest such
cases in Texas history. By the 1990s, the price of silver
dropped as low as $4/ounce.

1981 – Solidarity's Warning Strike

In what has been called the largest strike in the history of
Communism, the Polish labor union Solidarity
(Solidarność) called a four hour national warning strike on
March 27, 1981, to protest the use of violence by the
government against labor leaders. At least 12 million
workers struck, shocking the Polish government because
there were only 9 million members of Solidarity. Tensions
were high, and there was concern that a real strike planned
for March 30 would lead to civil war. An agreement
between Solidarity and Poland's Communist government
postponed the strike and led to some reforms, especially
in the area of police brutality.

1998 – Viagra® Approved

The first drug approved for the treatment of male erectile disfunction, Viagra® (sildenafil citrate), was approved by the US Food and Drug Administration on March 27, 1988. Advertised on television by notables including former US senator and presidential candidate Bob Dole and footballer (soccer player) Pelé, it became hugely popular, with annual sales reaching nearly US$2 billion. The drug was originally studied for treatment of high blood pressure and angina pectoris, when researchers noticed a rather unusual side effect. Some athletes use Viagra as a performance enhancer, and it has also been shown that powdered Viagra can extend the shelf life of cut flowers by as much as an additional week. Viagra is also used in the treatment of pulmonary arterial hypertension and altitude sickness, and a 2006 study showed that it helps treat jet lag recovery in hamsters.

2002 – Passover Massacre

In the deadliest attack against Israeli civilians during the Second Intifada, a Hamas suicide bomber attacked a Passover seder at a hotel in Netanya, Israel, on March 27, 2002, killing 30 and injuring 140.

"American Homestead Winter," a Currier & Ives print, for the birth of Nathaniel Currier, March 27, 1813

Who Was Born on March 27?

Art and Illustration

Carl Barks (March 27, 1901 – August 25, 2000)

Creator of Scrooge McDuck, Carl Barks labored in anonymity for many years, known to fans only as "The Good Duck Artist" before his identity became known to comics fans. He was dubbed "the Hans Christian Andersen of comic books" by the legendary artist Will Eisner, and in 1987 was one of the first three inductees into the Comic Book Hall of Fame.

An *Uncle Scrooge* panel drawn by Carl Barks
(© and ® Walt Disney Company)

Edward Steichen (March 27, 1879 – March 25, 1973)

Photographer Edward Steichen took the first modern fashion photographs and was the highest paid photographer in the world in the 1930s. He won an Academy Award for Best Documentary for the 1944 film The Fighting Lady.

Nathaniel Currier (March 27, 1813 – November 20, 1888)

Lithographer Nathaniel Currier partnered with James Ives to create Currier & Ives, the most prolific and successful lithography company in America. Over 7,500 images represented every aspect of American life. Selling for prices ranging from 5¢ to $3, they were an inexpensive and hugely popular source of home decoration. Today, original Currier & Ives prints are highly collectable.

Engineering and Architecture

Elsie MacGill (March 27, 1905 – November 4, 1980)

Elsie MacGill was the world's first female aircraft designer. She designed the Maple Leaf Trainer II and oversaw industrial engineering for the production of the Hawker Hurricane for the Royal Air Force. Known as the "Queen of the Hurricanes" for streamlining production and designing special cold weather solutions for the aircraft, her efforts produced over 1,400 Hurricanes for the war effort.

"Queen of the Hurricanes" comic book story about Elsie MacGill

Mies van der Rohe (March 27, 1886 – August 19, 1969)

Famous for his aphorism "Less is more" and "God is in the details," architect Ludwig Mies van der Rohe is considered one of the pioneers of modern architecture and is the developer of the Second Chicago School. He was the last director of the famed Bauhaus school in Berlin and head of the architecture department Chicago's Illinois Institute of Technology. His minimalist designs can be seen in Chicago's IBM Plaza (left), New York's Seagram Building, and Washington's Martin Luther King Jr. Library, as well as in smaller commissions like the Farnsworth House and the McCormick House, the latter of which has been incorporated into the Elmhurst Art Museum. He also designed furniture, including the Barcelona chair and the Brno chair.

Henry Royce (March 27, 1863 – April 22, 1933)

English car designer Henry Royce partnered with Charles Stewart Rolls to found the Rolls-Royce company.

Baron Haussmann (March 27, 1809 – January 11, 1891)

During the reign of Napoleon III, civic planner Georges-Eugène Haussmann oversaw a comprehensive rebuilding of the city of Paris in the 1860s, destroying the old medieval city to create a new one with wide boulevards, a new water and sewer system, as well as numerous public buildings. The immense project (2.5 billion francs in 1860, the equivalent of US$520 million at the time, or US$14 billion today) caused a major financial crisis in France, but led to the beautiful city we see today.

Paris c. 1890

Government and Politics

Cyrus Vance (March 27, 1917 – January 12, 2002)

Cyrus Vance was US Secretary of State during the administration of President Jimmy Carter. He previously served as Secretary of the Army and Deputy Secretary of Defense. Later in life, he served as Special Envoy of the Secretary-General of the United Nations for Croatia and Special Envoy to Bosnia.

James Callaghan (March 27, 1912 – March 26, 2005)

James Callaghan was prime minister of the United Kingdom from 1976 to 1979, and is the only politician in British history to have served in all four of the Great Offices of State: Prime Minister, Chancellor of the Exchequer, Home Secretary, and Foreign Secretary.

Letters

Patrick McCabe (March 27, 1955 –)

Patrick McCabe's novels *The Butcher Boy* and *Breakfast on Pluto* have both been turned into films.

Frank O'Hara (March 27, 1926 – July 25, 1966)

Writer, poet, and art critic Frank O'Hara shared the 1972 National Book Award for Poetry for his posthumous anthology *The Collected Poems of Frank O'Hara*.

Dick King-Smith (March 27, 1922 – January 4, 2011)

Children's author Dick King-Smith is best known for his 1983 work *The Sheep-Pig,* adapted as the 1995 movie *Babe.*

Military and Exploration

Brian Jones (March 27, 1947 –)

Brian Jones co-piloted the first successful uninterrupted circumnavigation of the globe by balloon on the Breitling Orbiter 3 in a 1999 flight that lasted nearly 20 days. He received the Harmon Trophy, the Hubbard Medal, and the FAI Gold Air Medal for his achievement. The Breitling Orbiter 3 gondola can be seen in the Smithsonian Institution's National Air and Space Museum.

Rudolf Christoph Freiherr von Gersdorff (March 27, 1905 – January 27, 1980)

German Generalmajor Freiherr (Baron) von Gersdorff tried and failed to assassinate Adolf Hitler by suicide bombing in 1943; later that year he discovered the mass graves of the Katyn Forest massacre victims in Russia.

René Fonck (March 27, 1894 – June 18, 1953)

French World War I aviator René Fonck was the top Allied fighter ace of the war, and remains the all-time Allied Ace of Aces with 75 confirmed victories and a probable total of at least 100.

Adolphus Greely (March 27, 1844 – October 20, 1935)

US Army officer and polar explorer Adolphus Greely is one of the few people to receive the Medal of Honor for peacetime service. He led the Lady Franklin Bay Expedition, which reached Ellesmere Island, the northernmost point in Canada. Becaue planned resupply efforts failed, nineteen of Greely's 25-person crew died. He later served as Chief Signal Officer of the US Army and as military commander following the San Francisco earthquake.

Music

Fergie (March 27, 1975 –)

Stacy Ann Ferguson under her stage name Fergie was lead vocalist for The Black Eyed Peas and a highly successful solo artist.

Mariah Carey (March 27, 1970 –)

Singer Mariah Carey (right) was named as the best-selling female music artist of the millenium in 2000. She has had more number one singles (18) than any other solo artist. She has a five-octave vocal range.

Tony Banks (March 27, 1950 –)

Keyboardist Tony Banks was a founding member of the progressive rock group Genesis and one of only two members who have been with the band through its entire history. As a member of Genesis, he was inducted into the Rock and Roll Hall of Fame in 2010.

Mariah Carey

Janis Martin (March 27, 1940 – September 3, 2007)

Rockabilly and country singer Janis Martin was known as the "Female Elvis" for her on-stage dance moves. Her 1956 hit "Will You Willyum" sold over 750,000 copies.

Mo Ostin (March 27, 1927 –)

President of Warner Records, Mo Ostin signed The Beach Boys, Neil Young, Paul Simon, and Van Halen, among many others, and built Warner into the largest recording company in the world. In 2003, he was named to the Rock and Roll Hall of Fame.

Mstislav Rostropovich (March 27, 1927 – April 27, 2007)

Soviet cellist and conductor Mstislav Rostropovich (Мстисла́в Ростропо́вич) is considered to be one of the greatest cellists of all time. He left the Soviet Union in 1974 and became musical director of the US National Symphony Orchestra in Washington, DC.

Sarah Vaughan (March 27, 1924 – April 3, 1990)

Jazz singer Sarah Vaughan was known as "The Divine One." She received the George and Ira Gershwin Award for Lifetime Musical Achievement and several of her recordings are in the Grammy Hall of Fame,

Ben Webster (March 27, 1909 – September 20, 1973)

Known as "The Brute" or "Frog," Ben Webster is considered one of the most important "swing tenor" saxophone players. He was the tenor sax soloist for the Duke Ellington Orchestra from 1935 to 1943.

Pee Wee Russell (March 27, 1906 – February 15, 1969)

Jazz clarinetist Pee Wee Russell progressed from Dixieland to swing, bebop and free jazz in his long career. He was inducted into the Big Band and Jazz Hall of Fame in 1987.

Sarah Vaughan (Photo: William P. Gottlieb)

Ferde Grofé (March 27, 1892 – April 3, 1972)

Composer, arranger, and pianist Ferde Grofé best known work is his 1931 composition Grand Canyon Suite. He was nominated for an Academy Award for his score to the 1944 film *Minstrel Man*.

Patty Hill (March 27, 1868 – May 25, 1946)

Nursery school and kindergarten teacher Patty Hill is known for co-writing the song "Happy Birthday To You" with her sister Mildred Hill.

Performing Arts

Holliday Grainger (March 27, 1988 –)

English actress Holliday Grainger played Lucrezia Borgia in the Showtime series *The Borgias* and Estella in the 2012 film version of *Great Expectations*.

Jason Narvy (March 27, 1974 –)

Jason Narvy played "Skull" Skullovich in the *Power Rangers* television and movie franchise from 1993 to 2012.

Nathan Fillion (March 27, 1971 –)

Nathan Fillion played the title role on the TV series *Castle* and the lead role in the cult television series *Firefly*.

Nathan Fillion (Photo: Raven Underwood)

Elizabeth Mitchell (March 27, 1970 –)

Elizabeth Mitchell was Dr. Juliet Burke on *Lost* and starred in *The Santa Clause 2* and *The Santa Clause 3*.

Pauley Perrette (March 27, 1969 –)

Pauley Perrette played Abby Sciuto on the television series *NCIS*.

Kevin Corrigan (March 27, 1969 –)

Kevin Corrigan is known for his role as Uncle Eddie on the sitcom *Grounded for Life*.

Quentin Tarantino (March 27, 1963 –)

Director Quentin Tarantino's films include 1992's cult hit *Reservoir Dogs* and the 1994 classic *Pulp Fiction*. He has earned two Academy Awards, two Golden Globe Awards, two BAFTA Awards, and the Palme d'Or.

Xuxa (March 27, 1963 –)

Brazil's most famous celebrity, Xuxa (Maria da Graça Xuxa Meneghel) is known as the "Queen of Kids" for her popular children's programming. She has 130 gold albums, 52 platinum albums, and 10 diamond albums and is listed by Forbes as one of the world's 40 highest-paid entertainers.

Maria Schneider (March 27, 1952 – February 3, 2011)

Maria Schneider is best known for her role opposite Marlon Brando in the 1972 film *Last Tango in Paris*.

Michael York (March 27, 1942 –)

Michael York was Tybalt in Franco Zeffirelli's 1968 film adaptation of *Romeo and Juliet*, D'Artagnan in the 1973 version of *The Three Musketeers*, the title character in *Logan's Run*, and Basil Exposition in *Austin Powers: International Man of Mystery*.

Jerry Lacy (March 27, 1936 –)

Jerry Lacy played multiple roles on the cult TV series *Dark Shadows* and had roles on numerous soap operas including *As the World Turns* and *The Young and the Restless.* He played Humphrey Bogart in the Broadway show and film *Play It Again, Sam.*

Julian Glover (March 27, 1935 –)

Glover played General Veers in *The Empire Strikes Back,* the villain in *For Your Eyes Only,* Walter Donovan in *Indiana Jones and the Last Crusade,* and Grand Maester Pycelle in the television series *Game of Thrones.*

David Janssen (March 27, 1931 – February 13, 1980)

David Janssen (right) is best known as Dr. Richard Kimble in the 1960s television series *The Fugitive,* and also starred in *Richard Diamond, Private Detective; Harry O;* and *O'Hara, U. S. Treasury.*

Anne Ramsey (March 27, 1929 – August 11, 1998)

Actress Anne Ramsey is best known for her role as Danny DeVito's mother in the 1987 film *Throw Momma from the Train,* for which she received an Academy Award nomination for Best Supporting Actress.

Fred Foy (March 27, 1921 – December 22, 2010)

Radio and television announcer Fred Foy is best known for his introduction of *The Lone Ranger* ("Return with us now to those thrilling days of yesteryear...") and also narrated radio's *The Green Hornet* and *Challenge of the Yukon.*

Richard Denning (March 27, 1914 – October 11, 1998)

Richard Denning starred in the 1954 film *Creature from the Black Lagoon* and 1957's *An Affair to Remember.* He played Lucille Ball's husband on the radio program *My Favorite Husband,* but was replaced by Ball's real-life husband Desi Arnaz for the television version, called *I Love Lucy.*

Gloria Swanson (March 27, 1899 – April 4, 1983)

Best known for her portrayal of Norma Desmond in the 1950 film *Sunset Boulevard,* Gloria Swanson successfully made the transition from the silent film era, where she was nominated for the very first Academy Award for Best Actress.

She had a long affair with Joseph P. Kennedy, father of the 35th US president, who financed several of her films. She also hosted the 1948 live television series *The Gloria Swanson Hour* and played herself in an episode of the TV sitcom *The Beverly Hillbillies*.

Gloria Swanson from the 1919 film *For Better, For Worse*

Public Figures

Edwarda O'Bara (March 27, 1953 – November 21, 2012)

Edwarda O'Bara slipped into a diabetic coma in 1970, and remained in a coma until her death 42 years later. Wayne Dyer's book *A Promise is a Promise* is about her mother Kathryn O'Bara, who remained with her daughter until her own death in 2008. Her father died in 1976 working three jobs to pay for her care.

Science and Technology

Karl Mannheim (March 27, 1893 – January 9, 1947)

Hungarian-born sociologist Karl Mannheim is one of the founding fathers of classical sociology.

Wilhelm Röntgen (March 27, 1845 – February 10, 1923)

German physicist Wilhelm Röntgen won the first Nobel Prize in Physics for his discovery of x-rays. Element 111, roentgenium, is named for him.

Sports

Buster Posey (March 27, 1987 –)

San Francisco Giants catcher and first baseman Buster Posey was named National League Most Valuable Player for 2012.

Robert Guerrero (March 27, 1983 –)

Boxer Robert Guerrero has earned world championships in welterweight, lightweight, and featherweight categories.

Danny Fortson (March 27, 1976 –)

Basketball power forward and center Danny Forton played for the Denver Nuggets, the Boston Celtics, the Golden State Warriors, the Dallas Mavericks, and the Seattle Supersonics from 1997 to 2007.

Randall Cunningham (March 27, 1963 –)

NFL quarterback Randall Cunningham played for the Philadelphia Eagles from 1985 to 1995, and after a year as a football analyst for TNT, he played for the Minnesota Vikings, the Dallas Cowboys, the Baltimore Ravens, and again for the Eagles. He received the Bert Bell Award for Professional Football Player of the Year in 1990.

Robbie Haines (March 27, 1954 –)

World champion sailor Robbie Haines won a gold medal as skipper of his Olympic sailing team in the 1984 Summer Olympic Games in Los Angeles.

Lynn McGlothen (March 27, 1950 – August 14, 1984)

Pitcher Lynn McGlothen played for the Boston Red Sox, the St. Louis Cardinals, the San Francisco Giants, the Chicago Cubs, the Chicago White Sox, and the New York Yankees in a career that spanned 11 seasons.

Mike Curtis (March 27, 1943 –)

Linebacker Mike Curtis played for the Baltimore Colts, the Seattle Seahawks, and the Washington Redskinns in his career from 1965 to 1978. He was named AFC Defensive Player of the Year in 1970.

Cale Yarborough (March 27, 1939 –)

One of only two NASCAR drivers to win three consecutive championships, Cale Yarborough was named one of NASCAR's 50 Greatest Drivers in 1998 and inducted into the NASCAR Hall of Fame in 2012.

Rita Briggs (March 27, 1929 – September 6, 1994)

Catcher Rita Briggs played for the All-American Girls Professional Baseball League from 1947 to 1954, and achieved the all-time single season record for most games played by a catcher in 1948.

Herb Stein (March 27, 1898 – October 25, 1980)

Herb Stein was a college and professional football player. At the University of Pittsburgh, he was a consensus All-American and was named to the College Football Hall of Fame in 1967. His NFL debut came in 1922 with the Buffalo All-Americans and was part of the 1925 Pottsville Maroons team that won the NFL championship only to have it taken away for a disputed rules violation.

Miller Huggins (March 27, 1879 – September 25, 1929)

Miller Huggins (right) played second base for the Cincinnati Reds and St. Louis Cardinals from 1904 to 1916, and subsequently managed the Cardinals and the New York Yankees. During his Yankees

HUGGINS, CINCINNATI

tenure, he managed the "Murderers' Row" teams that included Babe Ruth and Lou Gehrig, leading them to three World Series championships. He was elected to the National Baseball Hall of Fame in 1964.

"Maison aux Escaliers," by M. C. Escher

Who Died on March 27?

Art and Illustration

Dick Giordano (July 20, 1932 – March 27, 2010)

Comic book artist and editor Dick Giordano estalished the superhero characters for Charlton Comics, which were originally slated to be used in Alan Moore's *Watchmen* miniseries (later a movie of the same name). When the rights could not be resolved, Moore created new characters loosely based on the Charlton superheroes for the series. Giordano later served as executive editor of DC Comics.

M. C. Escher (June 17, 1898 – March 27, 1872)

Dutch graphic artist M. C. Escher is known for his drawings of impossible constructions.

Sir Gilbert Scott (July 13, 1811 – March 27, 1878)

Architect Sir Gilbert Scott designed, built and renovated over 800 building in England. Some of his important projects include the Albert Memorial, the Midland Grand Hotel, and the St. Mary's Cathedrals in Glasgow and Edinburgh.

Business

Jack Dreyfus (August 28, 1913 — March 27, 2009)

Money manager Jack Dreyfus founded Dreyfus Funds, which pioneered direct marketing to consumers. His paternal grandfather was a first cousin of the Alfred Dreyfus famous for his role in the 19th century Dreyfus Affair.

Kiichiro Toyoda (June 11, 1894 – March 27, 1952)

Kiichiro Toyoda (豊田 喜一郎) inherited Toyoda Automatic

Loom Works from his father, and decided that his company should branch out into the automobile business. The company he led later became better known as Toyota Motor Corporation.

Government and Politics

Irving R. Levine (August 26, 1922 — March 27, 2009)

NBC news correspondent Irving R. Levine reported from over twenty different countries in his long career, and was the first American television reporter accredited in the Soviet Union.

Lyn Nofziger (June 8, 1924 — March 27, 2006)

Lyn Nofziger was a conservative political consultant, serving as a White House advisor to US Presidents Richard Nixon and Ronald Reagan, and as Reagan's press secretary when he was governor of California.

Simon Bradstreet (March 18, 1603/4 – March 27, 1625)

Simon Bradstreet was the last governor of the Massachusetts Bay Colony, which became the Dominion of New England by order of King Charles II in 1684. A political moderate, he supported such ideas as freedom of speech in the heavily Puritan colony. His famous descendents include US Supreme Court justices Oliver Wendell Holmes Jr. and David Souter, US President Herbert Hoover, and actor Humphrey Bogart.

James VI and I (June 19, 1566 – March 27, 1625)

When English monarch Elizabeth I died without children, the next in line for the throne was the King of Scotland, James VI, son of Mary, Queen of Scots, first cousin to Queen Elizabeth I and herself a claimant to the English throne. When James VI of Scotland became King of England, he was the first person of that name to occupy the English throne, making him King James I of England and Ireland and King James VI of Scotland at the same time, although Scotland and England remained separate countries until 1707.

The reign of King James VI and I was known as the Jacobean era. In literature, it was a continuation of the Elizabethan era, with Shakespeare and other literary luminaries continuing to write. In politics, there was conflict between the King and Parliament, and the infamous Gunpowder Plot took place during his reign. Internationally, his reign saw the first English efforts to colonize North America; Jamestown, Virginia, is one of the many places named for him. He authorized a new translation of the Bible into English, known as the Authorized King James Version, still in widespread use today. He was succeeded by his second son, Charles I, whose conflict with Parliament led to the English Civil War, the establishment of Oliver Cromwell's Commonwealth, and his own execution.

James VI and I by John de Critz the Elder, 1606

Letters

Paul Williams (May 19, 1948 – March 27, 2013)

Music journalist Paul Williams founded the first magazine of rock criticism, *Crawdaddy*, and was considered a leading authority on Bob Dylan, Brian Wilson, and Neil Young. He authored 25 books. Williams was a long-time friend of science fiction writer Philip K. Dick, and served as executor of Dick's literary estate. He died of early onset Alzheimer's disease, attributed to a 1995 bicycle accident.

Stanisław Lem (September 12, 1921 — March 27, 2006)

Polish author Stanisław Lem was called "the most widely read science fiction writer in the world." His books have appeared in 41 languages. He is best known for his 1961 novel *Solaris*, which has been made into a movie three times.

Paul Zindel (May 15, 1936 – March 27, 2003)

Playwright and novelist Paul Zindel is known for his Pulitzer Prize-winning drama "The Effect of Gamma Rays on Man-in-the-Moon Marigolds" and his 1969 novel *My Darling, My Hamburger.*

Henry Adams (February 16, 1838 – March 27, 1918)

Historian Henry Adams was the grandson of US President John Quincy Adams and the great-grandson of US President John Adams. He is known for his nine-volume *History of the United States During the Administration of Thomas Jefferson*, but especially for his memoirs, *The Education of Henry Adams*, published after his death. That work won the Pulitzer Prize and was named by The Modern Library as the top English-language nonfiction book of the twentieth century.

Performing Arts

Farley Granger (July 1, 1925 – March 27, 2011)

Actor Farley Granger is best remembered for starring in two Alfred Hitchcock films, 1948's *Rope* and 1951's *Strangers on a Train*.

Art James (October 15, 1929 – March 27, 2004)

Art James hosted over a dozen game shows in his long career, including *Pay Cards!*, *The Joker's Wild*, *Classic Concentration*, and *Tic-Tac-Dough*.

Billy Wilder (June 22, 1906 – March 27, 2002)

Filmmaker Billy Wilder is one of only five people to have won Academy Awards as producer, director, and writer of the same film (1960's *The Apartment*). His many classic films include 1955's *The Seven Year Itch*, the 1959 *Some Like It Hot* (both starring Marilyn Monroe), and 1954's *Sabrina*. He received the Life Achievement Award from the American Film Institute, the Irving G. Thalberg Memorial Award, and the National Medal of Arts.

Milton Berle (July 12, 1908 – March 27, 2002)

Comedian Milton Berle was the first major American television star, hosting *Texaco Star Theater* from 1948 to 1955. He was known as "Uncle Miltie" and "Mr. Television" at the height of his fame.

Dudley Moore (April 19, 1935 – March 27, 2002)

Known to American audiences as Bo Derek's co-star in the 1979 romantic comedy *10* and as the drunken hero of the 1981 film *Arthur*, for which he received an Academy Award nomination, Dudley Moore first came to prominence as a member of the *Beyond the Fringe* comedy troupe and then for his long partnership with fellow Fringe comic Peter Cook. Moore was also an accomplished pianist. His composition "And the Same to You," a parody of classical music using the theme from the "Colonel Bogey March," can be easily found on YouTube.

Aldo Ray (September 25, 1926 – March 27, 1991)

Aldo Ray acted in such films as 1952's *The Marrying Kind*, 1955's *We're No Angels* alongside Humphrey Bogart, and 1958's *God's Little Acre*.

Ralph Bates (February 12, 1940 – March 27, 1991)

Ralph Bates acted in the long-running British comedy series *Dear John* and in a number of Hammer horror films, including such cult classics as *Taste the Blood of Dracula* and *Dr. Jekyll and Sister Hyde*.

Jack Starrett (November 2, 1936 – March 27, 1989)

Jack Starrett is best known to modern audiences for his role as Gabby Johnson in the 1974 Mel Brooks film *Blazing Saddles*, and as Deputy Art Galt in 1982's *First Blood*. He acted in several biker films and directed two: *Run, Angel, Run*; and *Nam's Angels*.

Eve Meyer (December 13, 1928 – March 27, 1977)

Pin-up model Eve Meyer was the wife of sexploitation filmmaker Russ Meyer, appearing in such films as *Operation Dames* and *Eve and the Handyman*, before becoming her husband's producer on such films as *Beyond the Valley of the Dolls*. She died in the Tenerife disaster, where she was a passenger on Pan Am Flight 1736.

Diana Hyland (January 25, 1936 – March 27, 1977)

Diana Hyland was a regular on the daytime soap opera *Young Doctor Malone* and the nighttime soap opera *Peyton Place* and won an Emmy for her role in *The Boy in the Plastic Bubble*. She played the wife of Dick Van Patten in *Eight is Enough* for the first four episodes just prior to her death.

Public Figures

Easley Blackwood, Sr. (June 25, 1903 – March 27, 1992)

Contract bridge player Easley Blackwood Sr. developed the Blackwood convention used in bridge bidding, and is a member of the American Contract Bridge League Hall of Fame.

Madeline Astor (June 19, 1893 – March 27, 1940)

American socialite Madeline Astor, second wife of John Jacob Astor IV, survived the sinking of the *RMS Titanic* in 1912, in which her husband perished.

Science and Space

Yuri Gagarin (March 9, 1934 – March 27, 1968)

Cosmonaut Yuri Gagarin (Ю́рий Гага́рин) became the first human in outer space on the Vostok 1 orbital flight, April 12, 1961. He died in the crash of a MiG-15 training jet he was flying.

Yuri Gagarin

James Dewar (September 20, 1842 – March 27, 1923)

Chemist and physicist James Dewar is best known as the inventor of the Dewar flask, originally designed for scientific and engineering purposes, but later turned into a commercial product under the brand name "Thermos bottle."

Sports

Hjalmar Andersen (March 12, 1923 – March 27, 2013)

Norwegian speed skater Hjalmar Andersen was the most successful athlete in the 1952 Oslo Olympics, taking home three gold medals.

Joe Start (October 18, 1842 – March 27, 1927)

One of the most famous baseball players from the earliest days of the sport, Joe Start (left), nicknamed "Old Reliable," played first base for the Brooklyn Atlantics, the New York Mutuals, the Hartford Dark Blues, the Chicago White Stockings, the Providence Grays, and the Washington Nationals. After his playing days, he managed the New York Mutuals. In his 13 year career, he had 1418 hits, 854 runs, 544 RBI, and a .299 batting average.

The Month of March

"Up from the sea, the wild north wind is blowing
Under the sky's gray arch;
Smiling I watch the shaken elm boughs, knowing
It is the wind of March."

— "March," John Greenleaf Whittier

In ancient Rome, March was the first month of the year. As the first month of spring, in the Mediterranean climate it marked the beginning of the military campaign season. That's why March (Martius) is named in honor of Mars, the Roman god of war.

Although the first month of the year was moved back to January sometime during the transition of Rome from a kingdom to a republic (historians differ), March was the first month of the year in Russia until the end of the 15th Century, and is the first month of the year in many other cultures and religions.

In the northern hemisphere, March 1 marks the beginning of meteorological spring. In the southern hemisphere, March is the equivalent of September, making southern hemisphere March the beginning of autumn.

March is one of the seven months that have 31 days in it. March starts on the same day of the week as November every year, and except for leap years starts on the same day as February. March starts on the same day of the week as the previous June except for leap years, and in leap years starts on the same day as the previous September and December.

March in Other Cultures

The month of March has different names in different languages. Some nations use calendars other than the Gregorian, and their months may overlap with March.

- Arabic (Egypt, Sudan, Yemen): مارس (Māris)
- Chinese and Japanese: 三月

- Croatian: Ožujak
- Czech: Březen
- Finnish: Maaliskuu (earthy month).
- Greek: Μάρτιος
- Hebrew: מרץ
- Hindi: मार्च

- Korean: 3 월에 (3 wol-e)
- Old English: Hreþmōnaþ
- Polish: Marzec
- Russian: март
- Slovene: Sušec
- Ukranian: березень (birch tree)
- Vietnamese: 腼吧 (tháng ba)

March Superstitions

"Beware the Ides of March (March 15)!"

"March comes in like a lion and goes out like a lamb."

"April borrowed from March three days, and they were ill."

The first three days of March are unlucky "blind days." If rain falls on these days, farmers will have poor harvests.

Children born on Easter Day will be fortunate; children born on Good Friday are doomed to be unlucky.

"If Our Lord falls in Our Lady's lap/England will meet with a great mishap." (If Good Friday or Easter fall on Lady Day, March 25, the Feast of the Annunciation of Our Lady, national misfortune will befall.)

Clothes washed on Good Friday will never come clean.

Children should not climb trees on Good Friday.

Bread baked on Good Friday will never go moldy; eggs laid on Good Friday will no spoil.

Marriages that take place during Lent will have trouble.

"Married when March winds shrill and roar/Your home will be on a distant shore."

Good days to be married in March are March 3, 5, 13, 20, and 23. Which day? "Monday for wealth, Tuesday for health, Wednesday the best day of all, Thursday for losses, Friday for crosses, Saturday for no luck at all."

March Symbols

Birthstone
Aquamarine (left) and bloodstone, both representing faithfulness, courage, and friendship.

Birth Flowers
Daffodils (right), symbolizing rebirth and new beginning. Daffodils are also the 10th wedding anniversary flower.

March Events

Honorary Months

Presidents, Congresses, and nations around the world issue proclamations recognizing particular months to honor certain causes. These events generally fall in March. (All US unless otherwise noted.)

- American Red Cross Month
- Child Life Month
- Fire Prevention Month (The Philippines)
- Irish-American Heritage Month
- Colorectal Cancer Awareness Month
- National Caffeine Awareness Month
- National Celery Month
- National Cheerleading Safety Month
- National Flour Month
- National Frozen Food Month
- National Noodle Month
- National Nutrition Month
- National Peanut Month
- National Sauce Month
- Women's History Month (celebrated in Canada during October)

Women's Suffrage Demonstration 1917

"March Madness" (United States)

The NCAA Men's Division I Basketball Championship, popularly known as "March Madness" or the "Big Dance," is a single-elimination tournament to establish the champion college basketball team.

Moveable and Multi-Day Events

Some events take place over a specific week or time period. Start and finish dates may vary from year to year. Some events occur on different days each year (such as "fourth Saturday of a month").

Birkat Hachama (ברכת החמה) (Judaism)

According to the Talmud, the Sun was created at the vernal equinox position at the beginning of the Jewish month of Nisan, established by tradition as March 25 on the Julian calendar (see "On Names and Dates").

The Birkat Hachama, "Blessing of the Sun" is recited when the vernal equinox occurs at sundown on a Tuesday, which happens every 28 years. When the Julian calendar gave way to the Gregorian calendar in 1582, the date shifted forward, and continues to shift slowly forward by approximately a day per century.

Birkat Hachama took place on April 8, 2009 (14 Nisan 5769), and will occur next on April 8, 2037 (23 Nisan 5797).

Birkat Hachama at the Western Wall, 2009

Earth Hour (International)

On the last Saturday of March each year, households and business are urged to turn off all non-essential lights for one hour between 8:30 pm to 9:30 pm on each person's local time to raise awareness of the need to take action on climate change.

Meat-Free Week (Australia)

Meat-Free Week, the last week in March, promotes vegetarianism.

National Cleaning Week (US)

National Cleaning Week, the last week of March, reminds us to start our spring cleaning.

Pediatric Nurse Practitioner Week (US)

Pediatric Nurse Practitioner Week is celebrated during the last week of March.

Seward's Day (Alaska)

Seward's Day, celebrated on the last Monday in March, commemorates the signing of the Alaska Purchase Treaty on March 30, 1867.

Easter Season

The Christian holiday of Easter in Western Christianity is held on the first Sunday after the Paschal Full Moon following the March equinox, which is officially set at March 21 by church reckoning. Easter itself can therefore occur as early as March 22 and as late as April 25, but occurs most often in April. In Eastern Christianity, which uses the Julian calendar, Easter occurs between April 4 and May 8. This also sets the date for the various events that lead up to Easter, most importantly the events of Holy Week. (For an explanation of Julian and Gregorian dates, see "On Names and Dates.")

Passion Sunday

The fifth Sunday of the Christian season of Lent is known as Passion Sunday in various Protestant denominations and by some traditionalist Catholics. Sometimes, the sixth Sunday of Lent is referred to as Passion Sunday, but it is more commonly known as Palm Sunday. Passion Sunday starts the two-week Passiontide, which ends on Holy Saturday, the day before Easter, commemorating the day that Jesus's body was laid in the tomb. The fifth Sunday of Lent can occur as early as March 8 (though the next time it will be that early is in 2285 CE), and as late as April 11.

Palm Sunday

The moveable feast of Palm Sunday commemorates the triumphant entry of Jesus into Jerusalem, an event mentioned in all four gospels. In many Christian churches, palm leaves are distributed to the worshippers. The earliest date for Palm Sunday is March 15, and the latest is April 18.

Maundy Thursday

The Thursday before Easter is Maundy Thursday, when the Last Supper took place. Because of its relation to Easter, the earliest day it can occur is March 19, and the latest it can occur is April 22.

Good Friday

Good Friday, observed during Holy Week on the Friday preceding Easter Sunday, commemorates the crucifixion of Jesus and his death at Calvary. Because of its relation to Easter, the earliest day it can occur is March 20, and the latest it can occur is April 23.

Holy Saturday

Sometimes called Easter Eve or Black Saturday, Holy Saturday commemorates the day in which Jesus's body lay in the tomb. Some mistakenly refer to this day as "Easter Saturday," but that properly describes the Saturday following Easter, the last day of Easter Week. The earliest it can occur is March 21, and the latest it can occur is April 24.

La crucifixion by El Greco

Easter

Easter celebrates the resurrection of Jesus Christ on the third day after his crucifixion. In the liturgical calendar, Easter follows the season of Lent, and begins the period known as Eastertide, which ends on Pentecost Sunday. Easter is observed religiously in a morning service. In the U.S., it's also common to decorate Easter eggs and make Easter baskets of eggs and candy, often with the Easter bunny as a symbol. The White House traditionally hosts an egg hunt, and many communities have Easter parades. Easter customs around the world include bonfires (Cyprus, western Sweden), men spanking women with a ceremonial whip (Czech Republic and Slovakia), egg fighting (Bulgaria), cross-country skiing and reading murder mysteries (Norway), and children dressed as witches collecting candy door-to-door (other Nordic countries).

Easter Eggs

Easter Monday

In some Roman Catholic and Eastern Orthodox cultures, the Monday after Easter is celebrated as a holiday. It is also known as Egg Nyte, featuring egg rolling competitions and dousing other people with water that had been blessed with holy water the previous day at mass. Easter Monday is also celebrated as Family Day in South Africa. In Guyana, people fly kites that were made on Holy Saturday. In Portugal, it is known as the Anjo (Ivy) Festival, in which people picnic in the countryside.

Śmigus-Dyngus (Poland, Hungary, Czech Republic, Slovakia)

The Monday after Easter in Poland and in the Polish diaspora is known as Śmigus-Dyngus, or simply Dyngus Day in the US. Boys throw water over girls they like and spank them with pussy willows. Girls avoid getting wet by giving boys "ransoms" of painted eggs.

Easter Week (Western Christianity), Bright Week (Eastern Christianity)

The period from Easter Sunday to the following Saturday is known as Easter Week. In both Western and Eastern Christianity (where it's known as Bright Week), the resurrection continues to be celebrated in church services. Easter Tuesday is a public holiday in the Australian state of Tasmania.

The month of March, by Hans Thoma

March Zodiac Signs

From the perspective of someone on Earth, the Sun appears to move through the sky throughout the year, along a path astronomers call the ecliptic plane. The ecliptic plane is divided into twelve constellations, known as the zodiac, based on traditionally observed patterns of stars. On your birthday, you can't see your constellation, because it's in the daytime sky.

The zodiac was first developed by Babylonian astronomers about 2,500 years ago. Because they were unaware that the Earth wobbles like a spinning top (known as *precession*), they didn't make allowance for the fact that the Sun's path through the zodiac changes over time.

That means there are now two sets of dates for your birth sign. The *tropical* dates are the original Babylonian dates; the *sidereal* dates tell you where the Sun actually appears as it moves along its annual path.

For March 27, the tropical sign is **Aries**, and the sidereal sign is **Pisces**.

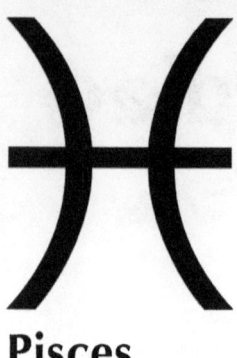

Pisces

Tropical February 20 to March 20
Sidereal March 15 to April 14

In the Roman legend of Venus and her son Cupid, they escaped the clutches of Typhon, known as the "father of all monsters," by transforming into fish and tying themselves together with rope. That's why the name Pisces is plural for fish. The constellation appears as a somewhat ragged "V" shape, representing the rope, with the "fish" located at the two rope ends.

In astrology, Pisces is a water sign, compatible with the other water signs Cancer and Scorpio, as well as with the earth signs Taurus, Virgo, and Capricorn. Pisceans are supposed to be imaginative, compassionate, unworldly, secretive, and escapist.

Aries

Tropical March 21 to April 19
Sidereal April 15 to May 15

In Greek mythology, Aries is a ram with golden wings and golden wool who rescued the twins Phrixus and Helle from certain death. Although Helle died in the rescue attempt, the grateful Phrixus sacrificed the ram to Zeus. The golden fleece from the sacrificed ram played a prominent part in the later myth of Jason and the Argonauts.

In astrology, Aries, a fire sign, is compatible with the other fire signs of Gemini, Leo, and Sagittarius, and to a lesser extent with air signs Scorpio and Libra. Arians are supposed to be adventurous, enthusiastic, quick-tempered, and impulsive.

Illustration by Edward Penfield

What Day of the Week is March 27?

On what day of the week does March 27 fall?

Surprisingly, this isn't an easy question. Because the calendar year is 365 days long (366 in leap years), it doesn't divide evenly by the seven days of the week.

Also, the Earth goes around the Sun in about 365-1/4 days, so a calendar tends to drift over time. That's why the same date falls on different weekdays in different years.

This is made even more complicated by a change in calendars that took place in 1582. Our modern calendar has its roots in ancient Rome, in a calendar reform conducted by Julius Caesar. Caesar commissioned mathematicians to attack the problem, and they came up with the idea of leap years, and thus standardized the calendar for centuries to come. This was called the Julian calendar.

Over time, however, the small errors in Caesar's calculation compounded. That's why Pope Gregory XIII commissioned the Gregorian calendar, used in most of the world today. Some countries converted in 1582, when the calendar was first developed; some converted later; other still haven't changed.

Gregorian and Julian aren't the only types of calendars. The Hebrew year, the Islamic year, and many other calendars are used in different parts of the world and among different people.

You can convert Gregorian dates to other calendars, including the Hebrew calendar, the Islamic calendar, and even the Mayan calendar by visiting the Fourmilab Calendar Converter at http://www.fourmilab.ch/documents/calendar/.

Chinese calendar systems are quite complex and have changed several times; a full discussion is far beyond the scope of this book. If you're interested, you can find information here: http://www.hermetic.ch/cal_stud/chinese_cal.htm.

A 50-year brass perpetual calendar.

On Names and Dates

Historians use "CE" (Common Era) and "BCE" (Before the Common Era) instead of the more common "AD" (Anno Domini, or Year of Our Lord) and "BC" (Before Christ), reflecting the fact that the year-numbering system established by the Gregorian calendar is used throughout the world in many countries not culturally Christian.

The CE/BCE designation dates back to at least 1708, and has been adopted as a standard by the United Nations and the Universal Postal Union. Because this series of books covers events and people of all nations and cultures, we use the CE/BCE terms.

The abbreviation "O.S." ("Old Style") on some dates refers to the fact that the Russian Empire did not switch from the Julian to the Gregorian calendar at the same time as the rest of Europe, and therefore some figures and events have two dates.

Also, in the Julian calendar in England in the 16th century, the year began on March 25 rather than January 1. To avoid confusion with Gregorian dates, dates between January and March were often written using both years.

People and events whose original names are not in the Western alphabet have their native names (where possible) in the appropriate script shown in parenthesis. If you are using an e-reader to access an electronic version of this book, all characters don't always display on all devices.

Cartoon by John T. McCutcheon

Copyright, Credit, and Contact

Follow Us

Our blog Dobson's Improbable History (http://improbhistory.blogspot.com) features short articles on events and people associated with each day, and updates several times each week.

You can also get a daily "What Happened In History" message and all the latest Timespinner Press news by following us on Facebook at https://www.facebook.com/TimespinnerPress. Our Twitter feed @SidewiseThinker links you to all our News of the Day.

Contact Us

Find an error or a format problem? Want information about the series, about us, or about when the volume for your special day might be available? Please email us at editor@timespinnerpress.com. (We also take requests if your special day isn't yet complete. Please give us at least six weeks' notice if possible.)

Sources

We owe a great debt to Wikipedia, which is our first stop for research. We attempt to make independent confirmation of all important dates and facts through a variety of other sources. Other sources we frequently use include the Library of Congress; "on this day" listings from *Encyclopedia Britannica*, the New York *Times*, and the BBC; and, of course, the always essential Google.

All art and photographs are either in the public domain, used under a Creative Commons license, or with a "fair use" justification, and most frequently come from Wikimedia Commons and the Library of Congress Prints and Photographs Division.

Attribution is provided where possible, or as requested by the copyright owner, or when there is particular historical significance, listed below. For information about any particular illustration or photograph, please contact us.

Credits

- The cover image of the National Cherry Blossom Festival was taken by Scott Bauer for the United States Department of Agriculture's Agricultural Research Service. It is in the public domain as a work of the US federal government.

- The illustration of the month of March on the back cover and in the frontispiece is from the French Gothic illuminated manuscript *Les Très Riches Heures du duc de Berry* by the Limbourg Brothers, Jean Colombe, and an intermediate painter whose name is lost to history. It is in the public domain because its copyright has expired.

- The photograph of a child looking at cherry trees along the Tidal Basin is from the Creative Commons Repository of Al Jazeera English, and is used here under CC-BY-SA 2.0.

- The photograph of cherry blossoms at the Washington, DC, Tidal Basin was taken by "Uberlemur," and is used here under CC-BY-SA 3.0.

- The photograph of the USS Constitution ("Old Ironsides") in Boston Harbor was taken by US Navy Journalist 1st Class Dave Kaylor in 2006. It is in the public domain as a work of the US federal government.

- The CGI rendering of the collision of the two Boeing 747s at Tenerife was created in 2008 by "Anynobody," and is used here under CC-BY-SA 3.0.

- The first panel of the *Uncle Scrooge* story "The Seven Cities of Cibola" was drawn by Carl Barks. It is both copyrighted and trademarked by The Walt Disney Company. It is used here under "fair use" provisions of the copyright law to illustrate a biographical entry on the artist. Its resolution is too low to make it suitable for the production of counterfeit works, it uses only a single panel of the comic story, and no comparable "free use" or public domain alternative exists.

- The lithograph "American Homestead Winter" by Currier & Ives is in the public domain because its copyright has expired.

- The opening page of the comic book story "Queen of the Hurricanes" is in the public domain because it was originally published in the United States between 1923 and 1963, and its copyright was not renewed.

- The 2004 photograph of Mies van der Rohe's IBM building in Chicago was taken by J. Crocker, who made the rights available for anyone to use for any purpose as long as proper attribution to the photographer is given.

- The 1890s view of Paris was scanned from the 1892 book *A Photographic Trip Around the World*, published by John W. Illiff & Company; the author and photographer are unknown. It is in the public domain because its copyright has expired.

- The 1998 concert photograph of Mariah Carey at Edwards Air Force Base is in the public domain as a work created by the US federal government.

- The 1946 photograph of Sarah Vaughan was taken by William P. Gottlieb, who donated this image as part of a collection of his jazz photographs to the Library of Congress in 1995. In accordance with the wishes of Gottlieb, all the photographs in the collection entered the public domain in 2010.

- The 2005 photograph of Nathan Fillion was taken by Raven Underwood, and is used here under CC-BY-SA 2.0.

- The 1963 publicity photograph of David Janssen as Richard Kimble from *The Fugitive* is in the public domain because it was published in the United States between 1923 and 1977 without a copyright notice.

- The 1919 publicity photograph of Gloria Swanson from the film *For Better, For Worse* is in the public domain because its copyright has expired.

- The 1911 American Tobacco Company baseball trading card of Miller Huggins is in the public domain because its copyright has expired. The original is in the collection of the Library of Congress, Benjamin K. Edwards Collection.

- The 1951 M. C. Escher lithograph "Maison aux Escaliers" is in the public domain because its copyright has expired.

- The portrait of James VI and I was painted around 1606 by John de Critz the Elder. It can be found in the Dulwich Picture Gallery. It is in the public domain because its copyright has expired.

- The circa 1950 publicity photograph of Milton Berle is in the public domain because it was published in the United States between 1923 and 1977 without a copyright notice.

- The official photograph of Yuri Gagarin is from the Great Images of NASA collection, and is in the public domain.

- The 1870 image of Joe Start is in the public domain because its copyright has expired.

- The photograph of aquamarine has been released into the public domain.

- The photograph of daffodils is by "Myrabella," and is licensed under the Creative Commons Attribution-Share Alike 3.0 Unported license.

- The 1917 Women's Suffrage demonstration comes from the Library of Congress, Prints and Photographs Division, LC-USZ62-31799 DLC, and is in the public domain because its copyright has expired.

- The 2009 photograph of Birkat Hachama at the Western Wall is by "Ingo," and is used here under CC-BY-SA 3.0.

- The painting *La crucifixión* by El Greco is located in the Museo del Prado. It is in the public domain because its copyright has expired.

- The photograph of Czechoslovakian Easter eggs was taken by Jan Kameníček, who has released the image into the public domain.

- The painting of März (March) is from the calendar book *Festkalender* by Hans Thoma. It is in the pubic domain because its copyright has expired.

- The 50-year perpetual calendar photograph is in the public domain.

- The cartoon by John T. McCutcheon is from his 1905 collection *The Mysterious Stranger and Other Cartoons by John T. McCutcheon*. It is in the public domain because its copyright has expired.

License Description and Terms

Aside from material purely in the public domain, photographs and other material in this book are used under specific licenses permitting free use, usually with an attribution requirement. For full text and terms of these licenses, click or enter the appropriate links below. If you believe there is an error in the copyright status or attribution of any of these images, please email us.

Michael Dobson

Timespinner
Press

www.ingramcontent.com/pod-product-compliance
Lightning Source LLC
Chambersburg PA
CBHW050430290526
45786CB00003B/1467